"A transformative Conversion Optimisation Strategy involves a multi-disciplinary team and processes that allow you to make intelligent, data driven decisions and validation based on your customers, to generate exponential business growth."

A Story of Untapped Potential :
The Growth Strategy That's Being Ignored

Copyright © 2015 PRWD.

All rights reserved.

First hardback edition printed 2016 in the United Kingdom. A catalogue record for this book is available from the British Library.

ISBN 978-0-9935249-0-5

No part of this book shall be reproduced or transmitted in any form or by any means, electronic or mechanical, including photocopying, recording, or by any information retrieval system without written permission of the publisher.

Published by PRWD
Printed in Great Britain

Although every precaution has been taken in the preparation of this book, the publisher and author assume no responsibility for errors or omissions. Neither is any liability assumed for damages resulting from the use of this information contained herein.

Acknowledgements

Paul Rouke - Author and Content Producer
Katie Kelly - Editor and Content Producer
Dante Naylor - Assistant Editor
Phil Williams - Senior Designer

Special thanks for all their contributions;

Bryan Eisenberg, Chris Goward, Craig Sullivan, Roger Dooley, Brian Massey, Angie Schottmuller, John Ekman, Peep Laja, Dr. David Darmanin, Linda Bustos, Bart Schutz, André Morys, Oli Gardner, Tim Ash, Talia Wolf and Michael Aagaard

PRWD

Follow @PRWD | #GrowthLeaders
optimisation@prwd.co.uk | 020 3813 4808

Contents

Foreword

The Experts

What's Holding Businesses Back
From Growing Through Optimisation?

Take Action

About PRWD

Be The Change

Foreword

Anyone who's implemented an intelligent A/B testing and optimisation strategy knows first-hand that it can be the biggest growth lever available to businesses. With thousands of case studies, reports, books and industry commentary on the subject, why is this strategy still underused by board level members looking for proven, methodical growth strategies?

My fellow Global Optimisation Group member and CEO André Morys from Web Arts said to me back in 2014, "we are the dirt under the fingernails of the digital industry". Having worked in the digital industry since 1999, I have to say the immaturity of optimisation processes and strategies within businesses still shocks me.

Optimisation will become a core element for the majority of businesses who really want to outpace their competitors and please investors, but until then there needs to be intelligent education and the beginnings of cultural transformation to bring businesses and senior decision makers up through the maturity scale. On reading (and sharing) this book, you may recognise some (or many) similarities with your business and with this understanding, you can begin making changes to gain a competitive advantage, mature your optimisation strategy and ultimately, deliver phenomenal business growth.

Paul Rouke
Founder & Director of Optimisation at PRWD

PRWD

The Experts

Bryan Eisenberg
Founder & CMO at IdealSpot

Bryan is the recognised authority and pioneer in improving online customer experiences and conversion rates. Bryan has helped companies such as HP and Intel as well as being on the advisory board of several successful start-ups. He is the co-author of the Wall Street Journal & New York Times bestselling books "Call to Action" and "Waiting For Your Cat to Bark?", and lauded by his peers as one of the world's leading digital marketers.

Chris Goward
Founder & CEO at WiderFunnel

Chris developed the LIFT Model™, a conversion optimisation strategy that has lifted one business' sales by $1million per month, with brands such as Google, eBay and Electronic Arts also benefiting. Chris is also a founding member of the Global Optimisation Group and author of best-seller 'You Should Test That!'

Paul Rouke
Founder & Director of Optimisation at PRWD

Paul is regarded as one of the UK's top experts in conversion optimisation, and developed the Growth Methodology™ focussing on user research and psychology, delivering significant results for clients including The North Face, Skyscanner and Schuh. Since 2009 Paul has been an international speaker, writer and trainer, and in 2015 developed the first conversion optimisation training course for Econsultancy. His agency PRWD are also the sole UK representative of the Global Optimisation Group.

Craig Sullivan
Director at Optimal Visit

Proclaimed 'User Experience champion', Craig has a wealth of experience gained by working with leading brands for over 15 years, including Lovefilm.com, Autoglass and John Lewis. Craig has delivered £30M in revenue for those he has worked with and speaks about conversion optimisation at conferences around the world.

Roger Dooley
Founder at Dooley Direct

Roger is a pioneer of splicing neuromarketing and conversion optimisation. He is the author of 'Brainfluence', founder of 'Neuromarketing' (the leading blog on the intersection of neuroscience and marketing), and regular contributor to Forbes through his channel 'Brainy Marketing'.

Brian Massey
Conversion Scientist at Conversion Sciences

Back in 2006 Brian launched U.S based agency, Conversion Sciences™ using the rigor of scientific data collection and testing as part of their conversion optimisation work. Between writing, presenting and managing the company, Brian also published 'Your Customer Creation Equation'.

Angie Schottmuller
Growth Marketing Consultant at Interactive Artisan

Angie's 16 years of marketing experience has been spent working with leading brands such as Nestle and The Home Depot. Named as one of the 'top 25 most influential conversion rate experts' and one of the 'top 10 online marketing experts to follow' by Forbes, Angie is the epitome of a digital marketing thought-leader.

Peep Laja
Founder of ConversionXL

Peep founded ConversionXL in 2011 to better spread the message of 'evidence based marketing'. He has developed and runs the world's most successful conversion optimisation blog at ConversionXL, as well as organising ConversionXL Live; an event where the world's brightest conversion optimisation minds meet annually.

Dr. David Darmanin
Founder & CEO of Hotjar

David is an award winning entrepreneur and consultant, who founded Hotjar in 2014, a company that offers analytics and feedback tools to better understand your site visitors. Currently, over 64,000 organisations in 184 countries use Hotjar to improve their online experience.

Linda Bustos
Co-Founder & Managing Partner at Edgacent

Linda is a permanent resident on many top marketers lists, providing expert opinion for the LA Times, Entrepreneur, Time, The New York Times and Forbes. Before co-founding Edgacent, Linda wrote for and managed 'GetElastic', the #1 subscribed Ecommerce blog on the internet.

Bart Schutz
Chief Psychology Officer at Online Dialogue

Bart is one of the world's leading persuasion psychologists and on the editorial board for the Netherlands Institute of Psychology. Founder and author of the renowned blog 'wheel of persuasion', Bart specialises in understanding and influencing online user behaviour.

André Morys
Co-Founder & CEO at Web Arts

André is a true conversion optimisation veteran. He started Web Arts in 1996 and it is now the largest conversion optimisation agency in Germany, working with many recognised brands. Alongside his 250+ conference appearances and numerous awards, André has written the often cited book 'Conversion Optimierung' and is a co-founder of the Global Optimisation Group.

John Ekman
Founder of
Conversionista

John set up Scandinavia's number one company in conversion rate optimisation. His experience spans internet software to i-gaming, leading him to become one of the most strategic thinkers in the world of conversion optimisation and member of the Global Optimisation Group.

Oli Gardner
Co-Founder at Unbounce

Oli is known as the man who 'has seen more landing pages than anyone else on the planet'. He is the co-founder of Unbounce the world leading tool for building, publishing and A/B testing landing pages. Unbounce currently boasts over 400,000 published pages and 31,439,232 leads generated.

Tim Ash
CEO at Site Tuners

Tim is founder of the international event, Conversion Conference and author of bestselling book 'Landing Page Optimization'. Tim has been carrying the conversion optimisation torch since the mid-nineties and his expertise has been sought out by Google, Facebook, American Express and many other leading brands.

Talia Wolf
Founder & CEO
at Conversioner

Previously working on CRO for The Next Web, Talia who speaks three languages, has taken conversioner international, running over 31,000 A/B tests for businesses. Talia is also a prolific speaker at events from Beijing to Madrid.

Michael Aagaard
Senior Conversion Optimizer at Unbounce

Michael is a certified 'Master of Web Copywriting' and has spoken as a keynote on the subject in 11 different countries. His reputation led him to be one of the foremost bloggers and conversion optimisation consultants before recently joining Unbounce as a Senior Conversion Optimizer.

What's holding businesses back from growing through optimisation?

"CRO should not be seen as a tactic – it needs to be embedded in the culture"

CRO should not be a tactic. CRO is also not a strategy for fixing short-term problems arising from narrow approaches to increasing customer sales. For CRO to be effective in an organisation it needs to be embedded in the culture.

Of course, you can get gains in conversion rates by applying the countless number of tools out there that offer "conversion boosts" that focus on petty details in customer interactions, but that doesn't solve the root cause. Ask yourself why is it that Amazon Prime customers convert 74% of the time on Amazon.com. That is according to a 2015 study from Millward Brown Digital. Compare that to 13% for non-prime members. The average for Ecommerce retailers is 3.1%, why is there a 2,200% difference?

Amazon's user interface isn't 22x better than average. Amazon's copy isn't 22x better than average. Amazon's design isn't 22x better than average. Amazon's prices aren't 22x better than average. Amazon isn't average and it doesn't think about average conversion rates or average customers. Amazon's stated goal is to be "the most customer-centric company on earth."

This fits with how we've defined conversion rate. "Conversion rates are a measure of your ability to persuade visitors to take the action you want them to take. They're a reflection of your effectiveness at satisfying customers. For you to achieve your goals, visitors must first achieve theirs." We first wrote that in 2001 and it's still true.

The companies that excel at conversions have evolved a culture of customer-centricity. And not at the manager or director level, but from the C-suite down. The best companies experiment. They absorb conversion rate optimisation learnings and incorporate them into strategic and operational changes. That makes them superior. And not just at fixing, but at creating customer experiences that delight their customers.

Bryan Eisenberg
Founder & CMO at IdealSpot
@TheGrok

"In a word: Silos"

In many companies, optimisation is siloed into a single department or role. It may be within the analytics department, or web sales, or marketing, or I've even seen it in IT.

But that approach relegates optimisation to a tactical practice. And that's why many companies are still testing button colour and form fields. Not that those things aren't important, but there's so much more potential.

Optimisation is a way of doing business. It's a strategy for embedding a test-and-learn culture within every fibre of the business. In a truly leading company, everyone looks at potential solutions to their challenges as hypotheses, and says "We should test that!"

Chris Goward
Founder & CEO at WiderFunnel
@chrisgoward

"Talking the talk but not walking the walk"

Most businesses talk about being customer centric or about the importance of putting the customer first. More and more businesses are now talking about how they are "doing conversion optimisation" or that optimisation is now one of their big strategic areas of focus as a business.

The truth is there is such a huge disconnect with what businesses say they are doing or focusing on, and what they are actually doing on the ground. Typically I see that this big disconnect comes in two main areas – 1) the budgets and resources that are made available to gain genuine, actionable customer understanding and to deliver intelligent, transformational optimisation don't match the intent 2) the quality of both the customer research and the optimisation that is being delivered don't live up to what's needed.

One specific example is quite simply that for the vast majority of testing that takes place, there is an absolute lack of an insight driven "Why?" behind what is being tested.

Another example is businesses who focus on the quantity of testing that they are delivering, without truly understanding the importance of the quality of testing as a foundation to their optimisation and growth strategy.

Globally there are only a handful of organisations that are truly walking the walk when it comes to growing their business through intelligent, insight driven, transformative optimisation. For the rest, the sooner they make that decision to start walking the walk, the more chances they have of taking market share and out-growing their competition.

Paul Rouke
Founder & Director of Optimisation at PRWD
@paulrouke

"I think that there is a Gartner Hype Cycle for A/B testing and that many companies end up stuck in the unproductive part, doing testing that doesn't shift the needle or more significantly, isn't teaching you anything for the effort"

We all go through a phase of burning rubber doughnuts in the car park of split testing. There's a lot of noise, smoke and light - but nobody is going anywhere. It feels like effort but it isn't being rewarded by learning.

The transition to learning and innovating from testing requires a maturity - about how problems and testing opportunities are discovered and prioritised, how test hypotheses are formed, shaped and built into live tests by the team. It also requires discipline - around how you instrument, run, measure and analyse your test results and how the pipeline of testing and the cycles involved can be optimised themselves. There are many factors that hold people back from productive testing and by sharing good testing practice (methodology), we can help every company going through the same place we've all been.

Craig Sullivan
Director at Optimal Visit
@optimiseordie

"A lack of focus
on the customer's
non-conscious mind"

While I do know some conversion optimisation experts who do understand consumer psychology and the principles of neuromarketing, many others tend to focus mostly on other approaches - tweaking pricing, feature lists, button sizes and colours, and so on. While by now most optimisers are aware of common psychological triggers, like social proof ("Join 23,000 subscribers!"), there are hundreds of possible non-conscious motivators that can be employed.

Today, there are many poorly optimised websites that even elementary CRO approaches can help. Once the basics are fixed, though, more sophisticated approaches will be needed to keep improving conversion rates. A key part of these better tactics will be a focus on the customer's non-conscious decision-making using brain and behavioural science.

Roger Dooley
Founder at Dooley Direct LLC
@rogerdooley

"The three-letter acronym (TLA) being CRO"
_____

The three-letter acronym (TLA) for the conversion optimisation industry is CRO, for Conversion Rate Optimisation. This is a sad moniker for a set of disciplines that offers so much promise.

The "conversion rate" is the number of transactions, or leads generated, divided by the traffic for a given period of time. It is a metric of optimisation, not the thing we are optimising. Anyone can easily increase the conversion rate of any ecommerce site by cutting all prices in half. However, this would bankrupt almost any business.

No, we don't optimise conversion rates, so CRO is a fundamentally flawed TLA. Despite the cool allusion to a black carrion bird, it cannot stand. We optimise revenue, growth, pricing, value propositions, images, navigation and more. Perhaps we're the Online Business Optimisation industry, OBO. That's taken, unfortunately.

Brian Massey
Conversion Scientist at Conversion Sciences
@bmassey

"Consumers buy your offering; internal teams buy your ideas. Which 'customer' converts better?"

Optimisation projects begin with convincing internal teams that status quo needs improvement. Yet marketers rarely approach internal teams as their 'customer' to aid the decision making process. With the buzz and challenge of learning the latest marketing, technology, analytics, and psychology tactics, it's rare for change management to be included and prioritised as a core competency. Not understanding the customer and recklessly proceeding with change is a guaranteed recipe for optimisation disaster. Ironically, the industry status quo needs improvement.

To champion optimisation means you're a perpetual driver of change. People naturally resist change in forms of avoidance, hostility, or even sabotage due to fear of potential uncertainty, discomfort, or loss of control. If you don't recognise, empathize and resolve change concerns amongst your project team up-front, your optimisation plan is doomed and your relationships are at risk. The team moves forward together, or eventually not at all.

How well do YOU understand your internal team as a customer – their needs, aspirations, concerns, influences, and barriers?

It's easy to scare off key stakeholders with too much change - new processes, new terminology, new tools, new risks, new skill requirements, new budgets, and new ways of thinking. Ensure meaningful growth and success for your optimisation efforts by strategically leading progressive change management (i.e. baby steps) and caring for the internal team as a customer. Measure and monitor optimisation support, resistance, and morale, and only introduce new changes when the team is ready and you're prepared to collaboratively guide, equip and support them to optimisation fruition.

Angie Schottmuller
Growth Marketing Consultant at Interactive Artisan
@aschottmuller

"Companies jump 'onto' optimisation but they don't get 'into' it"

We are seeing more and more and more companies go "all-in" on conversion optimisation. Tools are selected and purchased, staff are hired and trained. Priorities are set and the machinery starts churning out A/B tests. Great!

But…

They don't see results. Their expensive machinery does not have the ROI it needs. Should it be killed?

Possible conclusions:
- "A/B testing is not for us."
- "It's not the right thing to do."

My take:
"A/B testing is the right thing to do. You just don't do it in the right way."

So, what is the right way?
Pros use processes. Not tips. Not tactics. Not best practices. Processes.

Secondly – conversion rate optimisation needs dedicated "doers" for the daily testing grind. Yes - that's what it comes down to, the grind. When you're going to build something you need one architect, of course. But if your team is filled with a bunch of award-aspiring strategic egos only, and no plumbers, no electricians, no truck drivers, the team won't deliver.

If you look at it from the Gartner Hype Cycle point of view; companies have now started plunging from the "Peak of inflated expectations" into the "Trough of disillusionment". It'll be interesting to see how many make it to the "Plateau of productivity"?

John Ekman
Founder of Conversionista
@Conversionista

"Ever-increasing bullshit content about CRO"

People not knowing what they're doing is a big problem - especially when they think they DO know. Content people - not practitioners - write more and more articles about CRO to get more traffic, backlinks etc. - but they're really clueless about it. This bullshit content makes people believe CRO is a list of tactics, a swipe file. This creates false beliefs, unrealistic expectations and a naïve world view about the whole thing.

Peep Laja
Founder at ConversionXL
@peeplaja

"Best Practices – that are not 'best' for you"

It's become increasingly common for consultants, tools and services to write about best practices and tricks they recommend. This reduces optimisation to a list of hacks or shortcuts which clearly are not necessarily relevant to the audience.

We need to re-align optimisation to the user experience. Understanding our users, listening to their feedback and empathising with their needs is the only way to truly understand what needs to be optimised. First become your user – then optimise to create an experience you would be truly impressed by. This is the only way to 'win' in the long term.

Dr. David Darmanin
Founder & CEO at Hotjar
@daviddarmanin

"C-level executives need to oversee and ensure that capital investments consider not just the features and functionality an online store desires to launch with, or what is 'quickest and cheapest' in the short term, but consider the long-term costs to continually optimize the business"

A marketer's ability to leverage conversion optimisation is often made or broken by the ecommerce platform. When templates are hard-coded, it can be costly and timely to make even simple changes - especially when it requires outsourced development to implement these changes. If the marketer cannot make these changes his or herself and iterate quickly and at a low cost, the incremental gains of optimisation are more than offset by the costs to run them (especially if a site is responsive), which may force marketers to only run very simple tests, which don't bring a high enough return to justify continued investment in optimisation.

The ideal ecommerce platforms for testing flexibility typically are CMS-driven, where the marketer can control the front-end without IT, or multi-tenant, plug-and-play where features can be turned on and off by the marketer at zero cost, and nearly instantly without breaking code. And too often, these details are not considered nor included in RFPs and vendor selection processes.

Linda Bustos
Co-founder and Managing Partner at Edgacent
@edgacentlinda

"Embracing Optimisation caused hockey stick growth among lots of digitally mature companies. Yet lots of other companies still struggle to follow their growth paths"

A major cause is the embedding of 'optimisation' in an online marketing team, instead of embedding it as a 'company wide, data-driven & evidence everything' culture.

Exponential growth through optimisation is not about an online marketing instrument, it's about DNA. Top down; embracing optimisation should be a board level decision. Optimisation is often a way more effective business strategy than innovation… But it's the board that decides that everything should be tested for its effectiveness on the bottom line (as long as the statistical power allows for it). Besides marketing and sales also, CRO, IT, customer contact, etc. All should test their efforts and measurably improve the business. And while doing so, optimisation becomes your first hand customer intelligence, providing a competitive advantage since truly valid customer intelligence enters your companies' DNA.

Bottom up; the marketing and ecommerce teams that are currently 'just optimising web & app pages' should start focusing on growing their business as a whole. Start applying optimisation omni-channel and across all customer journeys and touchpoints.

And ultimately have a seriously senior consumer psychologist reign over all optimisation programs. Because only someone who understands conscious and sub-conscious brain processes, can turn the collateral exponential growth in customer intelligence into a long term competitive advantage.

Bart Schutz
Chief Psychology Officer at Online Dialogue
@BartS

"The ego of the optimisers makes 90% of test results a lie"
_____

Why? Most optimisers suffer from a cognitive bias called "confirmation bias". They work hard on analysis, hypothesis, concept and building an experiment. If you work hard for something, your mind wants to believe that it is true.

People start to select information according to their opinion - this effect is called "confirmation bias". What happens? As soon as the testing tool says "winning variation found!" they stop the test ... Because they want to believe their success. But this is much too early. I recommend to run tests 2-4 weeks to eliminate errors and noise in the sample to get valid results. The length of the sales cycles matters as well as campaigns and traffic sources - a lot of factors that most optimisers don't take into account!

André Morys
Co-Founder & CEO at Web Arts
@morys

"One of the biggest barriers to adopting a data-informed mindset, and a culture of testing & optimization, is a lack of trust, belief or empowerment coming down from the senior levels of businesses"

_____

Committing time, money and resources to optimization is an essential function of a growing company and shouldn't be shied away from. CEOs, senior management professionals, and the clients of agencies, should be taking a leadership position instead of resisting the requests of their teams. An unoptimized business is, well, just say it out loud like that. Do you want an unoptimized business? If you can't say no, you have no business being in business.

Oli Gardner
Co-founder at Unbounce
@oligardner

"Equating split testing with conversion rate optimisation"

Testing is a common component of CRO. And I am glad that some online marketers have belatedly gotten the "testing religion", as I call it. However, it is only a tiny part of optimisation. Basically testing is there to validate the decisions that you have made and to make sure that the business has not suffered as a result. But even if you are doing testing well (with proper processes, traffic sources, statistics, and methods for coming up with ideas), the focus should still not be exclusively on testing activities.

We have developed a detailed conversion maturity model to objectively evaluate whole companies along dimensions such as tools & technology, structure & organization, customer experience (of which the web is just a part), measurement & accountability, and culture & process. If you simply worry about testing velocity or other tactical outcomes you will miss the larger opportunity. Unless you see CRO as a strategic activity that has the potential to transform your whole business, you run the risk of it becoming simply a tactical activity that is a part of your online marketing mix. And that would be the biggest tragedy of all.

Tim Ash
CEO at SiteTuners
@timash

"The way people view and understand CRO"

Most companies address CRO as a means to optimise a specific KPI (for example - registrations) and nothing more. The majority of marketers run meaningless tests without any strategy or hypothesis and the results are hard to analyse and scale.

What marketers are missing is that conversion optimisation isn't about increasing just one KPI, it's about knowledge, a new way to learn about our customers better - their desires and goals, a new way to translate that knowledge into a better product and user journey that as a result increases revenues.

Testing call to action buttons or titles is nice, but these tests rarely change a thing and keep companies at a low level of optimisation. In order to change this and utilise CRO to its real extent, you have to run meaningful tests, build strategies, profile customers, ask the hard questions and be bold.

The more marketers focus on the elements they are changing rather than the strategy they are using, the harder it is to analyse test results and keep running tests. Since marketers aren't achieving the results they are looking for and have a hard time analysing their results, CRO is labelled as just another tool which may or may not have impact on a business and is not labelled for what it is - a gateway to our customer's emotional triggers, their desires and the way to finally creating a better product for our customers.

Talia Wolf
Founder & CEO at Conversioner
@TaliaGw

"Lack of insight and process"

Most marketers (and novice CROs) I talk to suffer from the same shortcomings I did when I was starting out in the optimisation industry.

I thought conversion optimisation and A/B Testing were one and the same. I did zero research and relied on testing to gain insight. At the time I didn't understand anything about test duration, sample size or segmentation—so my insight was basically useless. Through painful trial and error, I realised how backwards my approach was, and I decided to dedicate all my energy into learning how to do it right.

Today I have a solid process in place where I prioritize data-driven research much, much higher than A/B Testing. I think of testing as a final check to verify whether all the research I conducted and the hypotheses I crafted were in fact valuable and impactful. My mantra is "Testing is not an excuse to skip your homework!"

In my experience, process is king. It's the only way to effectively move from short-term tactics to long-term strategy.

Michael Aagaard
Senior Conversion Optimizer at Unbounce
@contentverve

Take Action

Here are 7 takeaways to ensure you implement a successful optimisation strategy into your business.

1. Put together an optimisation strategy with clearly-defined processes rather than thinking about tactics. Focus on the quality of what goes in and out of the process rather than quantity.

2. Understand your internal stakeholder's wants and needs. Employ change management and realise that implementing an optimisation strategy to the wider team will take time. To get the fullest effect, your optimisation strategy needs to have buy-in from board level and across the business.

3. Ensure you secure adequate and flexible budget and resources to run an ongoing, scaling strategy.

4. Refine and develop you processes for optimisation, don't stand still. Find out what methods work and ways to streamline insights & research gathering, testing process, knowledge sharing, hypothesis development and test implementation.

5. Get the right knowledge and expertise. Ensure you can get in-depth user research, you have access to data experts who can help with sample size and segmentation, psychology and copy experts, and developers who can help with test implementation across channels and browsers.

6. Ensure your strategy is genuinely customer-centric as well as hitting overall businesses objectives.

7. Ensure processes include communicating your work to the wider business and that learnings can be used in different online and offline channels.

About PRWD

We're a UK based conversion optimisation agency who have been optimising online experiences since 2004, but we don't stop there. Part of our DNA is to help be the change within businesses, driving transformational growth outside the remit of the website and uncovering learnings about your customers, proposition and competitors to drive revenue for your business.

We don't make guesses or let opinions dictate what to test, instead we put data and research at the heart of decision making. Making consumer research, data analysis and creative solutions the foundation of our Growth Methodology™, we're able to change user behaviour and transform the way your business does business.

We offer a range of services from fully managed conversion optimisation programmes, strategic maturity audits, moderated user research projects or data driven website redesigns.

Partnered with

Qubit — Deliver your big ideas

Optimizely SOLUTIONS PARTNER

VWO PREMIUM PARTNER

Sole UK Representative

GLOBAL OPTIMIZATION GROUP

Be the Change

PRWD